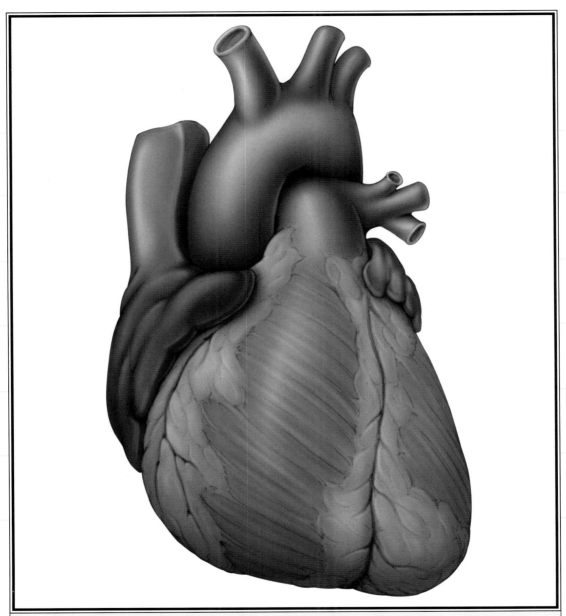

The heart is like the motor of the human body

THE *heart*

Anne Fitzpatrick

A⁺

Smart Apple Media

COPYRIGHT

Published by Smart Apple Media

1980 Lookout Drive, North Mankato, MN 56003

Designed by Rita Marshall

Printed in the United States of America

Pictures by Custom Medical Stock Photo (J.L. Carson), Corbis
(Ralph A. Clevenger, Rykoff Collection, E.H. Wallop), The Images Finders
(Jim Baron, John Petrus), Scott Leighton, Diane Meyer, Tom Myers, Photo
Researchers/Science Source (David Phillips)

Library of Congress Cataloging-in-Publication Data

Fitzpatrick, Anne, 1978- The heart / by Anne Fitzpatrick.

p. cm. — (The human body) Includes bibliographical references and index.

Summary: Explains how the heart moves blood through the body, how exercise
and a healthy diet keep the heart strong, and how to measure your heart rate.

ISBN 1-58340-308-6

1. Heart—Juvenile literature. [1. Heart.] I. Title. II. Human body systems
(Mankato, Minn.).

QP111.6 .F55 2003   612.1'7—dc21   2002030626

First Edition 9 8 7 6 5 4 3 2 1

THE *Heart*

CONTENTS

The Amazing Heart

People once thought that the heart was where thoughts, love, and courage came from. In fact, the brain is in charge of thinking and feeling. The heart has an even more important job. Without the heart, the brain and all of the body's other parts would stop working. The heart is the motor that keeps blood moving. Blood carries **oxygen** to every part of the body. The muscles, brain, and other body parts need the oxygen that the blood brings. They turn it into energy so they

The heart is sometimes considered a symbol of love

can keep working. It takes a lot of energy to keep the body healthy and active. ➤ The heart is the hardest-working muscle in the human body. It has to pump all the time to keep the blood moving. The heart never stops pumping blood, even while a person sleeps. A healthy heart will beat more than two billion times in a person's lifetime!

A mouse's heart beats about 500 times per minute. An elephant's beats about 25.

Even though you rest sometimes, your heart never does

We get energy from the oxygen carried in our blood

Heart at Work

The heart is connected to all parts of the body by tiny tubes called **veins** and **arteries**. Veins and arteries are like one-way streets. The veins carry blood toward the heart, and the arteries carry blood away from the heart. ➤ To pump blood, the heart contracts (makes itself smaller) and expands (gets bigger). It is a little like a hand making a fist and then relaxing, over and over again. When the heart contracts, blood is pushed out of the heart and into the

When the body is at rest, each heartbeat sends about two-thirds of a cup (158 ml) of blood into the arteries.

arteries. When it expands, blood trickles back in from the veins.

Blood makes two "loops" through the heart. First it is

pumped through the arteries to the lungs. There it picks up the

Tiny blood cells carry oxygen throughout the body

oxygen that the lungs breathe in from the air. Carrying the

oxygen, the blood travels through veins back into the heart.

Then the heart pushes the blood out into the arteries that take

it all over the body. The blood carries the oxygen to all of the

muscles and other body parts. Finally, it heads back through

the veins to the heart and starts the journey all over again.

The Beating Heart

Doctors use a **stethoscope** to listen to the heart

beating. They check to make sure the heart is healthy. The

heartbeat is the noise made by **valves** in the heart opening

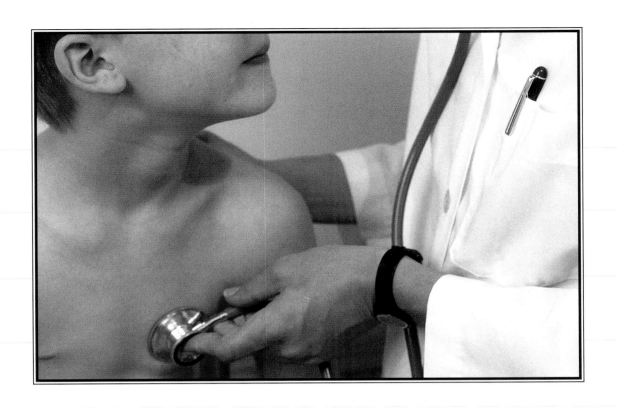

and closing. The valves are like little doors that open to let

blood in. After some blood goes through, they close to keep it

from trickling the wrong way. ➤ An adult's heart beats

Doctors use a stethoscope to listen to a person's heart

between 60 and 80 times per minute when at rest. A resting

10-year-old's heart beats 80 to 90 times per minute. The heart

slows down as it gets older. When a person exercises, the heart

beats two or three times faster. The **An adult's body contains about five quarts (4.7 l) of blood—about as much as one and a quarter gallons of milk.**

muscles need more oxygen because

they are working harder. The heart also

beats faster when a person is scared. It

sends extra oxygen to all of the body's muscles in case a

person has to fight or run away.

Your heart pumps faster when you exercise or play

Heart Health

Eating too much fatty food can clog the body's arteries. The stomach breaks food down into the vitamins and other good things that the body needs. The blood delivers them to the different parts of the body. When there is too much fat for the blood to carry, it can clog the

A drop of blood goes from the heart and lungs, out to a body part, and back in about 60 seconds.

arteries. If the blood cannot get through, the heart has trouble pumping. It is like a motor running without oil. This is called a heart attack. Heart attacks can cause a lot of damage to the

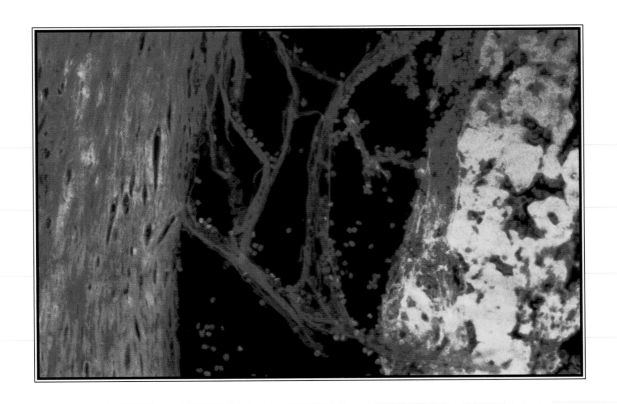

heart. ➤ The harder the heart works, the better it gets at

doing its job. People who exercise a lot have slower heart rates.

The heart is stronger, so it can pump more blood with each

An up-close look at an artery with a lot of built-up fat

beat. Regular exercise and a good diet are important to keep

the heart healthy. If the heart cannot do its job, all of the

body's other parts cannot get the oxygen they need. When the

heart is healthy and strong, the whole body feels better.

Swimming is great exercise for the heart and muscles

Measuring Heart Rate

Every time your heart beats, blood spurts into the arteries. You can feel these spurts by putting your fingers on an artery. This is called your pulse. By measuring your pulse, you can find out how fast your heart is beating. This is called your heart rate.

What You Need

A watch or clock
Paper and a pencil

What You Do

1. Place two fingers on the side of your neck, just under the jawbone, or on the inside of your wrist.
2. Count how many times your heart beats in 60 seconds. Write it down.
3. Run, jog, walk, or do jumping jacks for five minutes.
4. Find your pulse again and count it for 60 seconds. Did your heart rate go up after you exercised?

Kids have a higher heart rate than grown-ups do

INFORMATION

Index

Words to Know

arteries (AR-tuh-reez)—tubes that carry blood from the heart to the rest of the body

oxygen (AHK-si-jen)—an invisible gas in the air that people and animals must breathe to live

stethoscope (STEH-theh-skope)—an instrument that doctors use to listen to heart-beats

valves (VALVZ)—flaps in the heart that open and close to control the flow of blood

veins (VAYNZ)—tubes that carry blood from all parts of the body to the heart

Read More

Angliss, Sarah. *The Power Pack: Cardiovascular System*. Thameside Press, 1999.

Gold, John C. *Heart Disease*. Berkeley Heights, N.J.: Enslow Publishers, 2000.

Llamas, Andreu. *Respiration and Circulation*. Milwaukee: Gareth Stevens Publishing, 1998.

Internet Sites

BrainPOP Health: The Circulatory System
http://www.brainpop.com/health/circulatory

Open the Door to a Healthy Heart
http://www.healthyfridge.org/mainmenu.html

Way Cool Surgery
http://www.waycoolsurgery.com